Testamer.

BLACK MEN WALKING

methuen | drama

LONDON • NEW YORK • OXFORD • NEW DELHI • SYDNEY

METHUEN DRAMA
Bloomsbury Publishing Plc
50 Bedford Square, London, WC1B 3DP, UK
1385 Broadway, New York, NY 10018, USA
29 Earlsfort Terrace, Dublin 2, Ireland

BLOOMSBURY, METHUEN DRAMA and the Methuen Drama logo are
trademarks of Bloomsbury Publishing Plc

First published in Great Britain by Oberon Books Ltd 2015
Reprinted 2019
This edition was published by Bloomsbury, Methuen Drama 2021

A catalogue record for this book is available from the British Library.

ISBN: PB: 978-1-3502-6466-3

To find out more about our authors and books visit www.bloomsbury.com
and sign up for our newsletters.

Foreword

"There were Africans in Britain before the English came here"
(*Staying Power* – Peter Fryer)

I started Revolution Mix, an Eclipse movement, to challenge the notion that most Black stories in British theatre, film and radio were either imported or were the stories of new arrivals. I needed to put power in the hands of Black British writers. In 2015, conscious of a pervading erasure of Black British stories, I spent time with fifteen writers researching five centuries of this untapped vein of British history. This was the best starting point for a new body of work set across the country and the centuries. Eclipse is going to enjoy producing and sharing these new middle scale productions, radio plays and films in the run up to our 10th birthday.

Meeting local history teacher, Mark Hutchinson, who is also a founder member of Sheffield's Black Mens Walking Group was the catalyst for this work, the first Revolution Mix production. Joining these Yorkshire-men on their simple act of walking and talking in the Peak District once every month was as empowering as the numerous hidden Black Yorkshire histories I had discovered. Combining these two influences with the lyricism of Yorkshire based rapper, human beatboxer and theatre-maker Testament is what led to the development of *Black Men Walking*.

I hope that what is presented here is the framework of what was a formally challenging new production, that captured not only the spirit of the men we walked with but the hopes and ambitions of the Ancestors upon whose shoulders we stand.

In memory of Selwyn Hugh Walton (1935 – 2017)

Dawn Walton, Artistic Director – Eclipse

Introduction

Black Men Walking is a milestone for me. Thanks to all who walked this way before, to the passers-by and to the companions.

The piece has evolved and expanded in a way I would never have anticipated when I first met Dawn Walton and producer Emma Beverley one wet April evening, just getting off stage from a Saturday night show at the Leeds Central Library. We grabbed a bite to eat, chatted about Japanese food, which De La Soul album is the best, and found out about Dawn's groundbreaking vision for the Revolution Mix. She talked me through the idea of making a play using a real life black men's walking group based in Sheffield and drawing in over 500 years of British history. For me it presented an opportunity to dig through the crates of history, sample, remix, cut and crash stories together. Coming from the world of Hip-Hop, I guess much of what I do in theatre is viewed through that lens, that way of thinking/making. So after a few phone calls, I was in.

Months on, sat with muddy trainers on the huge rocks overlooking the Longshaw Estate and the ancient Padley Gorge, I found myself alongside the founders of 100 Black Men's Walk for Health. A group of inspiring men and women, whose intellect, camaraderie, humour and compassion stands as a warm provocation to me to be better.

Writing this play caught me at just the right time: as a new father; contemplating my own Anglo-African heritage and my adopted Yorkshire-ness. In these testing times we are I think required, collectively and individually, to face our complex relationship to a fractured national identity. *Black Men Walking* is an attempt to embrace the imprint we find here in the earth, hold it in tension and grow from it: to embrace our ancestors with all their richness of ingenuity, leadership, perseverance, courage, layers of complexity and contradictions of sorrow and hope.

We should celebrate. These stories are part of all of us.

Testament, 2018

Thanks to Dawn Walton for your vision and insight and giving me a remarkable opportunity I simply wouldn't have had otherwise. Shout outs to the critical insight of the legend and gent that is Ola Animashawun. Thanks to Steve Medlin for fascinating conversations. Bless ups to all the cast and team for their encouragement. Thanks also to Ric Watts and Suzanne Bell's for the last minute input. Thanks to the Royal Exchange Theatre for backing this project. Finally to Bex, I love you. Without you I wouldn't have been able to do this. Apologies if I've missed anything. Forgive me. I'm new here. T

Black Men Walking was first produced as a co-production between Eclipse Theatre Company and the Royal Exchange Theatre. It premiered at the Royal Exchange Theatre in Manchester on Monday 22nd January, followed by a national tour visiting fourteen cities.

Original Cast and Creative Team:

THOMAS	**Tyrone Huggins**
MATTHEW	**Trevor Laird**
RICHARD	**Tonderai Munyevu**
AYEESHA	**Dorcas Sebuyange**
Writer	**Testament**
Director	**Dawn Walton**
Designer	**Simon Kenny**
Lighting Designer	**Lee Curran**
Sound Designer	**Adrienne Quartly**
Movement Director	**Steve Medlin**
Writer and Musical Director	**Testament**
Voice and Dialect Coach	**Hazel Holder**
Dramaturg	**Ola Animashawun**
Casting Director	**Briony Barnett** CDG
Assistant Director	**Madeline Shann**
Company Stage Manager (on the book)	**Francesca Finney**
Production Manager	**Mark Carey, Venture Events**
Assistant Stage Managers	**Aniela Zaba, Elizabeth Rodipe**
Tour Technician	**Jake Channon**

He previously received an Olivier nomination in 2013 for *Constellations* at the Royal Court and Duke of York's, and in 2016 was nominated for a Knight of Illumination Award for *Orphee et Eurydice* at the Royal Opera House.

Adrienne Quartly – *Sound Designer*
Adrienne Quartly is a Sound Designer and Composer. She trained at City University and Central School of Speech and Drama. **Recent theatre credits include:** *A Raisin in the Sun* (Eclipse Theatre) *Opening Skinner's Box* (Improbable); *I am Thomas* (Told by an Idiot/NTS); *Bad Jews* (Theatre Royal, Haymarket); *Splendour* (Donmar Warehouse); *The Whipping Man* (Theatre Royal Plymouth); *The Ladykillers* (The Watermill); *Medea* (Gate); *Get Happy* (Barbican); *After Electra* (Theatre Royal Plymouth, Tricycle); *Ghost Train* (Manchester Royal Exchange); *Milked* (Soho Theatre, Pentabus tour); *Merit* (Theatre Royal Plymouth).

Steve Medlin – *Movement Director*
Steve Medlin Trained at Rose Bruford Drama School and with a host of physical theatre companies and artists including David Glass, Adrian Hedley and Theatre de Complicite, and is a founder member of Unclassified Arts. Stephen is a specialist in physical theatre and a regular actor/teacher with the BBC. He has appeared in television and film productions such as *Sweeney Todd, Jungle Run, Pump It Up, The Nutcracker, Moth* and *Sticks and Stones*. He has worked as Movement Director on a number of Eclipse shows including *A Raisin in the Sun, The Hounding of David Oluwale, There's Only One Wayne Mathews* and *One Monkey Don't Stop No Show* as well as Eclipse's set of *10by10* films, also productions for the Royal Court, Liverpool Everyman, The Young Vic, Theatre Centre and The Finborough.

Hazel Holder – *Voice and Dialect Coach*
As a Voice & Dialect Coach: *Barber Shop Chronicles, Angels in America, Les Blancs* and *Ma Rainey's Black Bottom* (National); *Guys & Dolls* (Talawa & The Royal Exchange); *Caroline, or Change* (Chichester Festival Theatre); Grimly Handsome, *Pigs & Dogs* and *Father Comes Home from the Wars* (Royal Court); *The Mountaintop, The Emperor and Cuttin' It* (Young Vic); *Twilight: Los Angeles* and *Eclipsed* (The Gate); **TV:** *In The Long Run, Poldark, No Offence, Broken, Dr Pepper.* **As a performer:** *Here We Go, As You Like It, Medea, Death and the King's Horseman* (National); *The Bakkhai* (Almeida); *The Tempest* (RSC); *The Bacchae* (National Theatre of Scotland / Lincoln Center, Broadway); *The Sleeping Beauty* (Young Vic, Barbican, New Victory, Broadway). Hazel was Resident Director for the premier London production of Dreamgirls 2016-2017

Ola Animashawun – *Dramaturg*
As an actor, director, and theatre-maker, Ola has been working in theatre for the past 30 years, with 20 of those 30 years dedicated to specialising in script development as a dramaturg, facilitator and script editor. Ola is an Artistic Associate of the Royal Court Theatre and alongside this role is also an Associate Artist, Dramaturg and Mentor for Theatre Absolute, Eclipse Theatre and Graeae Theatre. He also delivers regular playwriting programmes for Royal Central School of Speech and Drama, Belgrade Theatre and Central St. Martins – University of the Arts London. He is also a patron of Script Yorkshire.

Briony Barnett, CDG – *Casting Director*
Briony has worked in casting for over ten years in theatre, film and television. **Theatre credits include:** *Ben Hur* (Tricycle Theatre); *A Wolf in Snakeskin Shoes* (Tricycle Theatre); *Play Mas* (Orange Tree); *Ticking* (Trafalgar Studios); *The House That Will Not Stand* (Tricycle Theatre); *Handbagged* (West End); *The Colby Sisters, Handbagged* (Tricycle Theatre); *Fences* (Theatre Royal Bath); *One Monkey Don't Stop No Show* (Sheffield Theatres); *Not Black and White – Category B, Seize the Day, Detaining Justice* (Casting Assistant) (Tricycle Theatre). **Film credits include:** *Zero Sum;*

High Tide; What We Did On Our Holiday (Children's Casting); *10by10* (short films); *Travellers; Janet and Bernard; Final Prayer; Common People; Stop; The Knot; A Sunny Morning; Tezz; Value Life; Frequency; Conversation Piece; Our Time Alone; Love/Loss; Tears of a Son* (Casting Advisor); *Jhoom Barabar Jhoom* (Casting Assistant); *Love Aaj Kal* (Casting Associate); *Jhootha Hi Sahi* (Casting Assistant); *Red Tails* (Casting Assistant); *The Walker* (Casting Assistant). **Television credits include:** *Dickensian* (Children's Casting); *Inside the Mind of Leonardo; Just Around the Corner* (Children's Casting); *Outnumbered* (Children's Casting); *Spooks Series 5-8* (Casting Assistant); *The Fixer Series 1-2* (Casting Assistant); *Generation Kill* (Casting Assistant); *Kingdom Series 1-2* (Casting Assistant), *Five Days Series 1* (Casting Assistant); *Tsunami the Aftermath* (Casting Assistant).

Madeline Shann – *Assistant Director*
Madeline Shann is a theatre maker from Sheffield. She trained in Drama at Exeter University and Physical Theatre at Royal Holloway. Her own work includes one-woman show *Little Terrors* and mid-scale physical theatre piece *Sex In Real Life*. She is an associate artist at York Theatre Royal and has worked with Isley Lynn, Featherweight, and RashDash. In 2017 she was assistant director to Rob Hastie on *Of Kith and Kin* for Sheffield Theatres and the Bush.

Characters

THOMAS
Early 60s, Sheffield, Jamaican heritage

MATTHEW
Early 50s, Jamaican heritage

RICHARD
Early 40s, Ghanaian

AYEESHA
19 years old, Sheffield born and bred. Carribean
Heritage / possibly Mixed heritage

ANCESTORS
The spirits of all the black people who have walked
Yorkshire over the centuries
OR echoes in the landscape brought to life
OR the diverse essence of all the places we've come from, all
we've brought with us and all we have made
OR something else.

"Therefore, since we are surrounded by such a great cloud of witnesses, let us throw off everything that hinders…"

Hebrews 12:1

WE WALK PART 1

The three male actors perform "We Walk" a sung choral chant building to vocal breaths into ANCESTOR's first poem (The poem is broken up between the three male actors taking on the persona of the ANCESTORS unless otherwise stated).

ANCESTORS: We walk

We walk

We walk

We walk for freedom

We walk for honour

For beauty

For love

We walk out our identity

We walk for sanctuary

We walk to claim this land

We walk OUR land

We walk in the footsteps of kings

So heavy

Trumpets!

We are the faaaaannfaaaaaare!

Faaaanfare!

Faaanfare!

The declaration

The keyholders

Guildsman

Merchants

Healers

Emperors

We are the past

The future

We walk

Those that marched and those that were marched upon

And those that march
The writers and the written upon
And those that write
Though we are written into the landscape you
don't see us
We walked England before the English

We walk THIS land
The dales
The moors
The peaks
The vale
Dark summits
Orphaned valleys
Hidden gorges

We walk over the same waters
Across the Ouse
The Rother
The Ure
The Aire
Derwent
Mouth open to foreign sons
Become freshwater

We walk under the same stars
Under the same night sky
Celestial bodies
Absorbing innumerable refractions of colour
Into the same disparate blackness

Walking upon stone
Quartz
Jet
Mica
Feldspar

Knuckles cracked white and ashy
Stones in the drywall
Millstones to the mill

A commonality.
A humanity.
Lives woven through these Ridings
Home

Black in the white rose
God's own country
Even as we die here

Looking out onto a panorama of years
Despite death squinting through the vale in
readiness.
Now we see one
Who will fall
Into us

Space has always been here
Time has always been here
We have always been here!
And we walk

ACT ONE

SCENE 1

THOMAS: I mean, I've got the keys in my hand, stood in
the hallway. At the bottom of the stairs.
I've come in. Still got my coat on. Hello. Put
my bag down. Nobodys' said anything. Hello.
I can hear the TV's on in the lounge. It's
that property programme about Escaping to
the Country. She loves that show. You can't
really talk to her when that's on. It wasn't that
different when kids were here. They'd all be
busy doing their thing, y'know? But these
days... All the bedrooms are empty. They're
married, down south, doing I don't know
what... I used to talk to our Samuel about the
History sometimes. But now, all of them, they
just follow the crowd. See they never really
shared my interests. But if you don't know your
past, how is your future going to – "I know,
I know Dad!" they'd say. ...They never call
anymore anyway. They're all too busy. Well,
they do call...when they need help. And I
help. It's what fathers do, right?

Like my dad would do with me. Well he
tried... *(Dad voice.)* "What use a History
degree, son?" So I told him about John Blanke
and Catherine of Aragon, and all the stuff
that my school never told us. And he took a
moment, peered over his glasses... *(Dad voice.)*
"How dat ago pay fi a roof ova yu head?" ...
Well... A degree in history from Huddersfield
Polytechnic? *(Beat.)* I am going to change the
world... A calling... A destiny...If we can

4

grasp onto the past then... I mean... I tried...I
did... But then everything just –

"Is everything alright?" Dinner is in the
microwave and will I take the bins out. ...
And honestly I can't face it anymore! I've
been stuck sweating in traffic for two hours, in
my crappy Astra with broken cassette player,
listening to the football phone-in about how we
need more English players and I've realised
that everyday the commute is just a seething
bubble of rage, all the anger backs up for miles
with nowhere to go.

I mean, I've got the keys in my hand.
The wife says she wants us to go to church
more often. Oh God. And our Samuel's
become Muslim when we weren't looking.
And I can still hear my boss Sally telling
me I've dropped the ball on the employee
development reviews again. I've spent every
day working twice as hard as my colleagues to
get the same treatment. The promotion. Hell
man! I can't even afford to retire! Sally will be
paying for drinks tonight, but I'm never invited
to the pub, to the party, their homes, the
anniversary do... Too black... and now I'm too
old. ...Too old.

History! Perhaps its only purpose, is to let you
know when you're consigned to it.

I'm stood in the hallway. And I can't move.
She doesn't need me anymore. I mean...
And I have those type of thoughts again.
And I can't move.
Then all of a sudden it makes sense.

I mean, I've got the keys in my hand, stood in
the hallway. And now, I can hear them. All of
them. Calling for me.

And I'm out the door.

SCENE TWO

*End of March. On the edges of the Peak District. An overcast Yorkshire on a
mild Saturday morning out in the country. Grindleford Café at the bottom
of a hill, down from the Padley Gorge woods.*

MATTHEW is outside the café on the phone.

MATTHEW: Oh come on darling... Please... Don't be like
                  that... No. It's too late, I'm here now. ...I told
                  you I was going. *(Pause.)* For Pete's sake it's
                  once a month! Just-just for me to be myself for
                  a... Can't I have that? What's the problem?
                  No. No... I'm Richard's lift. What?...He's
                  part of the group... Of course I care! Don't be
                  ridiculous! I-I didn't mean ridiculous, sorry.
                  Sorry darling. Well, my phone'll be turned off
                  until we get back so if you can just wait until...
                  There's no need for name calling! ...Vicky, I'll
                  keep my phone with me alright? Reception
                  might not be great, so text me if you can't get
                  through... I'm sure we can work this out, so just
                  text me if... *(Vicky hangs up.)*

                  Saints preserve us.

RICHARD emerges from the Café with a coffee and plastic bag full of snacks.

RICHARD: You know Matthew, for a small cafe in such
                  a secluded spot, they've actually got a good
                  selection. Are you sure you don't want
                  anything?

MATTHEW: *(Trying to compose a text.)* No, it's fine Richard...

6

RICHARD:	Chocolate bar?
MATTHEW:	*(Still texting.)* No thanks.
RICHARD:	Snickers? How about a Double Decker?
MATTHEW:	*(Still texting.)* No thanks.
RICHARD:	Twix?
MATTHEW:	*(Still texting.)* No thanks.
RICHARD:	Not even a little Kit-Kat?
MATTHEW:	I'm fine, thank you Richard. I've brought fruit. *(Returns to phone.)*
RICHARD:	Ah. *(Beat.)*
RICHARD:	The guy in the café mentioned the weather too you know?
MATTHEW:	Oh.
RICHARD:	I hope it stays like this. Especially as I missed our last walk.
MATTHEW:	Oh yes. *(Stops with phone.)* The convention. How was it?
RICHARD:	It was pretty awesome actually. "StarTrek Con". Captain Jean-Luc Picard himself was there! Patrick Stewart – you know he's from Yorkshire?
MATTHEW:	Hm. Did you meet him?
RICHARD:	Well it was very busy so I didn't quite meet him. But I saw him… It was very exciting – you know there were over three thousand people there?
MATTHEW:	Sounds good.

RICHARD:	Oh yah, and very nice people. ...I think.
MATTHEW:	Who did you go with?
RICHARD:	Ah, I just figured what the hell, get out of the flat, do something different!. So... I went on my own.
MATTHEW:	On your own?
RICHARD:	Yah. Cool.
MATTHEW:	Right.

MATTHEW returns to texting.

RICHARD:	*(Beat.)* Hey, I've left my phone in your glovebox is that okay? I've been looking forward to today. Get away from the tech for a while. Too much phone y'know...and my Mom's been calling me all the time this week. Non-stop.
MATTHEW:	*(Still texting.)* That right?
RICHARD:	*(Sighs.)* Hmm.
MATTHEW:	*(Still texting.)* Right.
RICHARD:	Away from the screens. Out... Into nature.

Beat.

THOMAS enters preoccupied.

THOMAS:	*(To himself.)* Right... *(To the others.)* Now then gentlemen!
MATTHEW:	Not like you to be late Thomas.
THOMAS:	What you on about? I've been out already.
MATTHEW:	You've been out already?

THOMAS: Yes.

MATTHEW: Are you okay?

THOMAS: Nowt wrong here lad. I – I'm ready for
             anything! How are you?

MATTHEW: Well, erm…

THOMAS: You alright there Richard?

RICHARD: I'm okay thanks. Yah, good to be back out here.
             I missed it last month with the –

THOMAS: Oh yes, your Star Trek.

RICHARD: It was great, real fun, you know? They even
             had –

THOMAS: Nice to see you lad. Very nice. Now, seeing as
             there's not many here. We should knock it on
             the head today. Eh lads?

MATTHEW: Are you alright Thomas?

THOMAS: I'm fine! We're not all southern softies Matthew!

RICHARD: *(To THOMAS.)* Did you hear about the warning?

THOMAS: The what?

MATTHEW: The weather forecast? They said –

THOMAS: Oh yes, yes.

RICHARD: It'll be okay right? You sure it'll be safe?

THOMAS: Safe? It's Springtime! They don't know what
             they're on about half the time! I'm going! A
             little weather won't stop me. You lot go back.

RICHARD: No, weather won't stop us. Real Yorkshiremen!

THOMAS: Aye. Hm…

9

Beat.

MATTHEW: But just to be sure, we could –

Couple walk past.

THOMAS: Morning.

MATTHEW: Morning.

RICHARD: Hello.

THOMAS: *(About the walking couple.)* Looks like everyone's
                 retreating. Separate the wheat from the chaff
                 eh? *(Beat.)* Okay. So you're here are you?

MATTHEW: We are.

THOMAS: Today's a day of breakthrough. I can sense it.
                 We can push ourselves.

MATTHEW: Up to the rocks?

THOMAS: Past the rocks! Right up to the Roman Road up
                 to Whirlow and into the beyond lad! Boldly go
                 where no man has gone before, eh Richard?

RICHARD: Into the beyond?

THOMAS: Yes, we'll actually be crisscrossing in and out of
                 the Yorkshire border today lad – we'll be right
                 on the edge of God's country. You guys okay
                 staying out for a bit longer?

RICHARD: Oh yes. …And in The Next Generation, it's
                 "boldly go where no ONE has gone before".
                 They decided to be more egalitarian you see?
                 There's actually –

THOMAS: Right. *(To MATTHEW.)* What about you? Don't
                 you have to be back for 'kids?

MATTHEW: Um. Well... Vicky's taking them to her sister's actually...

THOMAS: Great. Destiny's a calling. The land cries out. If you listen close you can hear –

MATTHEWS phone goes off with a text.

MATTHEW: Sorry.

THOMAS: Honestly. You had to bring your phone? What's the point of us having rules if –

RICHARD: *(To MATTHEW.)* Y'know it WAS you who first told me about the rule –

MATTHEW: It's just – sorry. I need to sort some work stuff out...

THOMAS: Do you!?!

MATTHEW: Well, yes. I just need to be on...call... on this – today... Over the weekend period.

THOMAS: You can go home if you like.

Beat.

MATTHEW: I guess it'll be good to be out and about. A bit of space.

RICHARD: The brotherhood.

MATTHEW: Indeed.

THOMAS: Right then. *(Leaving.)* We walk.

RICHARD follows.

RICHARD: Yah, my phone's in the car Thomas.

THOMAS: Hm.

Beat.

RICHARD: Do you want a Kit-Kat? *(THOMAS walks on.)*...
                Hey, are you coming Matthew?

They walk.

SCENE THREE.

They've been walking for half an hour. THOMAS leads at a pace. RICHARD is trying to keep up. MATTHEW lags behind as he's been texting.

RICHARD: Hey Matthew?

MATTHEW: Yes?

RICHARD: I love these circular stones in the ground here.

THOMAS: Millstones.

MATTHEW: Ah yes, millstones.

THOMAS: You find them all round here. They're left over
                from the mills and quarrying. They were dug
                out, carved and then just left. Been here for
                hundreds of years.

RICHARD: Man and nature. Beautiful.

MATTHEW's phone goes off.

(Beat.)

MATTHEW reads his text. THOMAS and RICHARD watch him.

MATTHEW: Sorry... work.

THOMAS: How is Vicky?

MATTHEW: *(Finishing text.)* Er, great.

THOMAS: Hm.

RICHARD: *(To MATTHEW.)* How long have you been
                married?

MATTHEW:	Um… About nineteen years now.
RICHARD:	Really? Long time. You enjoy it?
MATTHEW:	Oh, it's…of course, er…
RICHARD:	What does she do?
MATTHEW:	Vicky used to be an artist. Well, she still is an artist.
RICHARD:	Okay.
MATTHEW:	Performance art really.
RICHARD:	Really?
THOMAS:	I never knew that.
MATTHEW:	Well, she mainly works with learning disabled kids these days.
RICHARD:	Oh. A fulfilling job eh?

THOMAS starts walking on at a pace.

MATTHEW:	Pretty much. I suppose.
RICHARD:	Hey, is this woodland area still Grindleford, Thomas?

THOMAS is silent.

MATTHEW:	*(To himself.)* He's off again.
RICHARD:	It's very pretty here.

Beat.

I can hear water.

MATTHEW:	Yes, it's down there. Padley Gorge. You have to be a bit careful around here. You can't see it, but a few yards that way, past those ferns,

	there some more of those millstones and then suddenly, almost hidden, there's a really, steep drop straight down "whumph" into the... uh.. gorge.
RICHARD:	I see. ...Hey, Thomas is pretty energised today isn't he?
MATTHEW:	And he says he's already been out.
RICHARD:	You know him better than me, but it's like he doesn't want to walk with us.
MATTHEW:	He doesn't sound right.
RICHARD:	He doesn't seem himself.
MATTHEW:	*(Goes after THOMAS.)* Thomas! ...Hang on Thomas!

THOMAS stops.

	Right, sorry to be a pain Thomas. But we're doing this TOGETHER aren't we? We're creating a safe space here. Unity. Right?
THOMAS:	Okay.
MATTHEW:	So we'll stick together a bit more?
THOMAS:	Hm... Fine. I need to pay my respects to the land.
MATTHEW:	Oh, ok, yeah, of course.

THOMAS turns his back on MATTHEW & RICHARD, unzips his fly and starts to urinate, where he stands.)

RICHARD:	Hey!
MATTHEW:	Oh really! What?
THOMAS:	What? It's a libation.

RICHARD: This is not the kind of libation we do in Africa.

(RICHARD and MATTHEW step away while THOMAS urinates. MATTHEW glances at his phone.)

RICHARD: A lot of pressure I guess?

MATTHEW: He'll be okay.

RICHARD: I meant your phone. Work?

MATTHEW: Oh no – well yes… It's fine.

RICHARD: I've been reading about all the pressure you doctors are under! You've got to remember why we do this! Get away from all the stress y'know?

MATTHEW: Yes.

RICHARD: Take advantage of our beautiful country eh?

MATTHEW: Do you miss home?

RICHARD: Home? Do you mean Sheffield?

MATTHEW: No sorry, I meant here compared with… where you grew up?

RICHARD: Oh.

MATTHEW: Y'know I'd really love to go to Ghana. I haven't even been to Jamaica yet.

RICHARD: You have family over there?

MATTHEW: Yes. I know I've got an auntie over there who's keen to see me and the kids. Mind you, Vicky says the kids are too young to go anyway… Do you visit much?

RICHARD: No… Actually, my mom has been pushing me to go back next week.

MATTHEW:	Next week! Wonderful! I imagine it will be good to go back.
RICHARD:	Back to what?
MATTHEW:	Oh… Perhaps –
THOMAS:	*(Out into the ether.)* The blood of our elders. Not so easily conquered.
RICHARD:	What's he doing?
THOMAS:	Ave vivas in deo.

MATTHEW and RICHARD runs over to THOMAS to investigate.

MATTHEW:	Thomas. Thomas? You alright?
THOMAS:	What? I'm rayt.
RICHARD:	What were you saying?
THOMAS:	Just.. uh…
MATTHEW:	Are you SURE you're feeling well?
THOMAS:	Will you give over and stop asking if I'm alright! Come on, are you ready?
MATTHEW:	We're ready!
THOMAS:	Onward then!

They walk.

	Right, lets go out of these woods and up the hills to the rocks.
MATTHEW:	Have you walked this route before Thomas? I mean the whole way round?
RICHARD:	Is it a steep walk?

THOMAS:	This one? Are you soft lad! It's tame, this one! Families do it. With their little kids! Remember when we did this two year ago Matthew?
MATTHEW:	I can't imagine there'll be kids up on the rocks today.
THOMAS:	Good, I'm not keen when they're up there hanging about. Playing their music. Doing I don't know what. ...Nuisance.
RICHARD:	How are your children?
THOMAS:	Oh, y'know. They're great. They're great... Just busy. ...I suppose. Doing their thing. ...But I'm busy too nowadays. Oh yes, very active.
RICHARD:	Sometimes I think about children. I'm getting on you know?
MATTHEW:	I'm sure you've got plenty of time.
THOMAS:	Is there no one on your arm at the moment? Haven't found your Uhuru yet?
RICHARD:	"Uhura" ...and she's in Star Trek: The Original Series, not Next Generation. Whereas "Uhuru" actually, is an African international socialist movement. It's quite cool.
THOMAS:	Right... So no luck then?

Beat.

RICHARD:	No, not really.

Spotting some passers-by.

THOMAS:	Morning.
MATTHEW:	Morning.
RICHARD:	Hello.

THOMAS: Keep up lad.

Beat.

Did you see her look at us then? Daft int'
it? You'll be going about your business and
someone will just look at you funny. Y'know,
like the way you can feel security guards
looking at you sometimes. I mean you forget,
and then all of a sudden someone just looks at
you funny.

MATTHEW: Not like the nod.

THOMAS: The nod! You know the other day –

RICHARD: The nod?

MATHEW: You know when you see another black person
and you sort of give that nod.

RICHARD: Oh yes, yes. *(Hears something.)* What bird is
that?

MATTHEW: A grouse I think.

THOMAS: Red grouse… Yeah, the other day this lad was
walking along. Near Waterstones in town. And
I give him the nod, y'know. And he just did
this.

THOMAS stops and screws up his face. They all stop and look at THOMAS.

RICHARD: A screwface?

THOMAS: A screwface! Exactly. *(They resume walking.)* A
screwface. The younger generation don't seem
to get it.

MATTHEW: I suppose millennials will have a different
experience won't they? The context has
changed somewhat –

18

THOMAS:	Hmmpf. Well. *(Puffing up a hill.)*

(Passer-by goes past.)

THOMAS:	Morning.
MATTHEW:	Morning.
RICHARD:	Hello.

(Beat.)

This is great isn't it?

MATTHEW:	You know Richard, funny this but – the other day someone in our surgery thought *I* was Ghanaian. *(MATTHEW starts to laugh expecting the others to join in – they don't.)*
RICHARD:	Really?
MATTHEW:	Perhaps when they see me – a black professional in the NHS, they just automatically assume I'm African!
THOMAS:	Complete lack of knowledge!
RICHARD:	*(To MATTHEW.)* Yes… Your face does have some typical Ashanti features. But as soon as you open your mouth, it's clear that you're really as English as Yorkshire Pudding! –
THOMAS:	An adopted Yorkshire pudding! He's Hertfordshire this one!
MATTHEW:	I've been here long enough! *(Pleased, to RICHARD.)* You think I have some Ghanaian features?
RICHARD:	Your nose for example –
THOMAS:	Ha! I'm sure African tribal variations won't have entered their mind! They just took one

19

look at you and can't understand you're born
and bred in this country!

That's Barnsley for you!

MATTHEW: I… Well, I take exception to that Thomas –

THOMAS: I tell you, I went there once or twice on a night
out as a lad. Every time I went there I was
offered out.

MATTHEW: It's changed a lot I'm sure –

THOMAS: I still don't like it. You'd get the train into
Barnsley market for car boot, only to be told to
"Go back where you came from!" – and they
didn't mean Pittsmoor! Kids have it easy these
days.

MATTHEW: That was a long time ago.

THOMAS: They don't know the half of what we had to
deal with. Football matches? Worst were derby
days.

RICHARD: Really?

THOMAS: When Wednesday used to play Barnsley? All
the fans – and then add a black face into the
mix?? Oh it were shocking. …South Yorkshire
Police looking on? Doing chuff all.

RICHARD: *(Kisses teeth.)*

THOMAS: But at least you'd be prepared for it. Even then,
sometimes it'd catch you.

RICHARD: What do you mean?

THOMAS: Matthew, do you remember Paul Canoville?

MATTHEW: *(Struggling to remember.)* Ah.

THOMAS:	He was fantastic. Do remember him? Chelsea. Yeah, yeah.
MATTHEW:	Eighties?
THOMAS:	Oh yeah. Way before we had Thomson or Chamberlain at Wednesday. One of the first black players — a big deal for us, that was. He came on for Chelsea when they played us in the League Cup and they treated him terribly.
MATTHEW:	Monkey sounds?
THOMAS:	Monkey sounds. Bananas. The works... Even his own fans. Terribly. There was a lad down MY road. A lad I'd played on the street with. I saw him and his dad going off to Hillsborough with the scarves and everything.
MATTHEW:	Hmm.
THOMAS:	The rattles. Remember them, big wooden things? They made a hell of noise. Then I noticed a banana sticking out of his coat pocket...
MATTHEW:	Terrible.
THOMAS:	And you think they're your mate, y'know and he thought we were monkeys. Monkeys! Eating bananas!... Y'know: "You're alright Tom. YOU'RE not one on them." You expect it from some people – but you don't expect it from someone you see about.

Beat.

MATTHEW:	Someone you are close to.

Silence.

THOMAS: Eating bananas!… Four-All it was. Canovile came on for the second half and scored straight off the bench! Eat that.

Beat.

(Musing.) You know what you should've told the ignoramus in your waiting room? You should've told him there are Africans buried in Barnsley from Roman times, 2000 years ago! Africans! – you'll like that, eh Richard? Shove that up their inbred dee-dars! – hey, we'll be coming up to the Roman road after the Rocks. Did you know –

RICHARD: *(Looking up the hill.)* Hey.

THOMAS: What?

RICHARD: What's that's up ahead?

THOMAS joins RICHARD staring.

THOMAS: Is that a car?

They all look.

MATTHEW: Police.

They all change demeanour.

THOMAS: *(Poshest voice.)* Hellooo officer.

WE WALK PART 2

ANCESTORS: We walk

Through treacherous lands
We walk with purpose
We walk with an army.
And so

He speaks
"Nunc se continet atque duas tantum res anxius
optat, panem et circenses!"
And now the people only hope for two things:
Bread and circuses.
He nods to himself
Reading his beloved poet Juvenal
Almost at the outpost.

Even in the mist he stands out
Even above the Centurions
His chest, a bronze heroic cuirass
Commander of nations, the emperor's crest
African blood in royal veins
There he is
Septimus
'Why have we stopped?' asks one of his sons
Looking out into the vapour
What's that up ahead?
Figures
Up there! The rocks!
Dismount! Horses to the rear! Shields!
Men change formation, compacting themselves
Voices!
This land still has echoes of the resolute
renegades
Remnants of the The Brigante tribes not yet
relented
British savage

But his generals are alert
Heedful of what happened to the disappeared
Ninth years ago
But the emperor himself has already overcome
so much

Greater battles are to come he thinks, looking
at his sons
Who will command unity out of the ranks?
Discord
Isn't so easily conquered
Death
Not so easily assuaged

And one day
He will not be here.
Which of these will bring unity?

SCENE FOUR

A hillside. MATTHEW, RICHARD and THOMAS have all stopped and take in the view…

RICHARD: Is that Sheffield?

MATTHEW: I think so.

THOMAS: No Sheffield's over there, Derby's down there.

RICHARD: Ah.

MATTHEW: Are we still in Yorkshire?

THOMAS: We're right on the edge. Will be heading into
                foreign territory soon.

MATTHEW: Those clouds look a little ominous.

THOMAS: See what happens when you leave Yorkshire?

   Beat.

                He was alright though, wasn't he?

MATTHEW: Yes, I think so.

RICHARD: I'm sure he approached us to genuinely warn us
                about the weather and the roads and so on.

MATTHEW: Yes.

Beat.

THOMAS: Still you think, don't you?

RICHARD: Yes.

MATTHEW: Yes.

Beat.

THOMAS: It's that feeling in't it?

RICHARD: Y'know, before I came here I didn't really
                realise I was black?

THOMAS: Eh?

RICHARD: Then you come here and people see you
                differently. ... That sense of suspiciousness.
                They hear your voice, their eyes glaze over
                and... you're a "black guy".

THOMAS: Yeah. Three BLACK guys eh?

MATTEW: Most people probably wouldn't even register
                they are doing it. When – um – I mean, the
                little comments and so on... But it's fine – it's
                fine, it's the way people view us.

THOMAS: We're the threat aren't we?

RICHARD: They promote that. Newspapers, television.

THOMAS: Well, you hear it all the time don't you? Let's
                see: which sounds more threatening to you eh?
                "The girl was accompanied by three men."
                (Beat.) Or: "The girl was accompanied by three
                black men?" *(Beat.)* ...Exactly.

MATTHEW:	Three black guys. On the Yorkshire moorland. Walking with our boots, woollen socks, a selection of brightly coloured bobble hats from Millets.
RICHARD:	Ha! The ironic thing is all the Yorkshire serial killers seem to be white. The Yorkshire Ripper, Myra Hindley –
MATTHEW:	I think Myra Hindley and Ian Brady were in Greater Manchester actually.
THOMAS:	Dunt matter where they were from. Tell you what, there wouldn't have been any of those serial killers if they knew there were black men out here roaming the countryside. They'd have seen us coming and crapped themselves!

They laugh.

Beat.

MATTHEW:	Still… He was alright wasn't he?
THOMAS:	All things considered.
RICHARD:	Yes. All things considered.
MATTHEW:	Thomas, it is getting a bit cold –
RICHARD:	Shall we turn back?
THOMAS:	Let's push on… Keep up if thee can gentlemen!

They go to leave.

WE WALK PART 3

ANCESTORS:	We walk To the next waypoint

The Miller
Bread!
The City Freeman
Out here on this rock
Highwaaaaays and by-waaaaaays
Over the same rock
Sandstone
Limestone
Gritstone

Long waistcoat, stocking worn over the knee
John Moore
"BLACK"
An AFRICAN man

Heading for home, tired
West of Padley Gorge
A day's ride from
His prosperous city of York
Having clasped hands with the quarrymen
Struck the bargain
For progress!
And build a mill
New millstones!
At last

He walks
And the city thrives again
In the face of bias against "unfree interlopers"
And the "limiting of foreigners."

Something pushes him on
As he pushes his burdensome circle
And still gives them what they need to make
their bread
John Moore
"BLACK"

One of the few able
To grind the barley
To pay wages
To have the means to buy the keys to the
freedom of York!
Only through a resilience
He pushes on
A sticking of hands, knuckles cracked white and
ashy
Who holds perseverance?
Freedom
Keys in our hands
He walks home
(THOMAS is walking.)

THOMAS: Oh.

ANCESTORS: Freedom
                  Keys in our hands

And THOMAS walks straight into next scene …

SCENE FIVE

THOMAS and MATTHEW walking uphill ahead of a struggling RICHARD.

THOMAS: *(Still talking to ANCESTORS.)* I mean, I got the
                  keys in my hand.

MATTHEW: Thomas?

THOMAS: Eh?

Beat.

MATTHEW: Thomas… Forgive me, you've been muttering
                  to yourself for the last five minutes and…

THOMAS: I'm rayt.

MATTHEW:	Just to check, you've not been restless or feeling irritable?
THOMAS:	I am now.
MATTHEW:	No anxious feelings?
THOMAS:	I left those down 'hill this morning – we walk!

Beat.

MATTHEW:	Aren't you worried about the weather?
THOMAS:	The darkened clouds are not the only skies.
MATTHEW:	What are you talking about?
THOMAS:	I know what I'm doing.
MATTHEW:	Tom. Where are you taking us?

THOMAS stops and stares at MATTHEW.

Beat.

THOMAS:	We've got to The Rocks.

THOMAS gestures toward The Rocks. They all sit down and get out bottles of water, taking in the land spread out in front of therm. RICHARD arrives last and is out of breath.

RICHARD:	Wow. I made it. That was steep eh?
THOMAS:	Get hydrated lad.
RICHARD:	I can't even see the woods with the mist down there. Are you sure it'll be alright?
MATTHEW:	*(Checks phone.)* …Let's see. My weather app says it's foggy.
THOMAS:	Well, I can see that!

MATTHEW: But it looks like it may be worse than we
                thought. *(Referring to the app on his phone.)* It's
                saying it's going to go down to zero...

THOMAS: That's no bother, we're prepared aren't we? I've
                got an extra fleece here if –

MATTHEW: It's talking about visibility.

THOMAS: Hmm.

RICHARD: It's going to be okay?

THOMAS: 'Course.

They continue drinking.

RICHARD produces a Kit-Kat.

RICHARD: Food. Hey, would either of you like a –

THOMAS
& MATTHEW: No thanks.

MATTHEW produces a banana and eats it. THOMAS sees him.

THOMAS: Oh really?

MATTHEW's phone rings. MATTHEW moves away to take the call.

                ...Exactly.

RICHARD: So big man, how's life?

THOMAS: Life...Death.

RICHARD: Hmpf! I've had enough of death.

THOMAS: No, no son. You've got to grasp it with both
                hands.

RICHARD: No thanks.

THOMAS: You'll see.

Beat.

RICHARD: My mom wants me to go back for a funeral. …
But I'm not going. It's okay I think. …My father
died… That's it…

THOMAS: Sorry lad.

RICHARD: I don't need sympathy. To be honest he's taken
enough of my time already.

THOMAS: Hm. I didn't really know my father until I came
here. I was five years old when I was sent for.
I can't remember much before Sheffield really
but I remember, just …the strangeness of him.
Big Man of the house. Sat in his armchair …
Still waters and that.

Funny, int'it? It's only when they're gone you
start talking to them.

(Beat.)

You weren't close?

RICHARD: No.

THOMAS: Still your Dad.

RICHARD: 'Dad?' He was my 'father' perhaps, but I didn't
really know him. …You remember when we
went to the Upper Derwent Reservoir?

THOMAS: Of course. Great day that.

RICHARD: Yah, that was the day I realised I had lived in in
the UK most of my life. It was so beautiful there
– I was deeply moved… Spiritual I think.

THOMAS: Hm.

RICHARD: And then I… *(Dismissive.)* Stupid.

THOMAS:	What lad?
RICHARD:	...I resolved to try and break the silence with my father. ...I sent him post card... Of the reservoir. ...And... A few words... He never even wrote back. ...Foolish.
THOMAS:	Well, you tried. How come you never knew him?
RICHARD:	My father was of that generation of Ghanaian who had had three 'wives'.
	My family was the one he supported the least. Yes, there was no doubt he liked us the least. He could be very cruel. Not even willing to try. And when I saw my half-brothers they were the ones to always have the new school uniform and the latest whatever... y'know? I said to my mom – we can let THEM go to the funeral.
THOMAS:	Oh... So you didn't see him much?
RICHARD:	He came only very rarely to see us. And she had to take three jobs to provide for us? Not good jobs. But she would not remarry or leave him! What woman would take that nowadays eh? She was still in love with him at the end I think. ...My mom says he wasn't at peace. I said, he had THREE families to find some peace. ...
(Beat.)	
	You know I have never even been into his house? Yah, he had a big house in a nice part of Accra – Achimota. I'd only ever seen from outside.
(Beat.)	

I don't owe him anything... My mom... She
won't be happy at all.

THOMAS: Well, when is it?

RICHARD: Next week. She's expecting me to contribute
too.

THOMAS: And you haven't told her yet?

RICHARD: It's just expected. *(Beat.)* You can bet he didn't
leave anything for my Mom.

Yet she will want me to pay for one of those
ornate fancy coffins. This is the burden of being
a Ga. You don't get this with the other tribes.
They don't have these extravagant funerals
to celebrate moving from one life to the next.
Hocus pocus! This nonsense – your ancestors
being with you!

THOMAS: Seems reasonable to m –

RICHARD: And just because I'm in the UK, they'll expect
me to pay for it all! Why should I dig into my
pocket to pay for a ridiculous coffin! I might as
well just go to Natwest, withdraw all my savings
and bury it in the ground! *(Clicks teeth.)* ...And
the longer they live, the more expensive the
funeral.

THOMAS: How old was your Dad?

RICHARD: Eighty-bloody-five years old!

THOMAS: Right. ...It's good that you're connected to the
old customs and traditions int'it though?

RICHARD: He wasn't even a proper Ga. He was half-
Ashanti! And he had that typical Ashanti
arrogance and disrespect. He couldn't even be
pleased for me when I got the job in England.

Always pushing me down, if the world didn't
run according to his will. He cut me off when
he heard I was coming here... All he ever had
for me was arrogance and disrespect. And
then... Nothing.

(Beat.)

He manages to be a bastard, even when he's
dead!

THOMAS: It's alright lad. ...Anger it – it can isolate you
can't it?

RICHARD: I know where I belong, and it's not there!

THOMAS: It's alright. ...We're here.

THOMAS and MATTHEW look out into the mist.

WE WALK PART 4

The ANCESTORS speak. Sometimes THOMAS joins them.

ANCESTORS: We walk.
We walk this fine line
We walk the blood of our elders!
We retrace our steps.
Blood lines,
Colour-lines
Walking between two selves

There we are.
William Darby
Coloured English 'well-to-do' gent
Grows up
And transforms
Into Pablo Fanque
His professional name

34

The man behind
Unsurpassed novelties
Magnificent assemblage of Historical
And Olympian
Entertainments
Proprietor of the greatest circus in the land!
Circuses!
(Overlapping.) Roll up.
Roll up!
Roll up!
Top hat
On horse back
Death defying acts
A crowd favourite

1854 a strange spring
He walks across the border
Returning across the Pennines
Into God's country
Preparing the big show
Where he himself would be buried
When his own circus caravan
Turned into a hearse
A funeral procession
Retracing his steps
When the immense weight of the crowd
Would line Leeds streets
In tribute
No longer walking alone
Here
In this Yorkshire
Where he once lost a son

SCENE FIVE

MATTHEW joins RICHARD & THOMAS after his phone call

THOMAS: *(To MATTHEW.)* Back with us are you now?

MATTHEW: Right! What's the matter with you Thomas?

THOMAS: I know oppression when I see it.

MATTHEW: What are you talking about? Look I think we'd
             better head back don't you?

THOMAS: That's okay with me.

MATTHEW: Good. …I'm relieved to be honest.

THOMAS: You two go.

MATTHEW: …Hang on!

RICHARD: Ay!

MATTHEW: Out with it Thomas! Has something happened?

THOMAS: Has something happened? Ha! Of course
             it's ALL happened. We walk the line of our
             ancestors! We walk our history! *(THOMAS starts
             readying himself to leave.)*

MATTHEW: Will you just give me a straight answer! – no
             history lesson, aphorisms or half the sodding
             Encyclopaedia Britannica for a ch –

THOMAS: Gentlemen. I'm going.

RICHARD: Where are you going?

MATTHEW: Thomas! We should NOT be out here any
             longe-

THOMAS: Look, I always said "We walk for freedom!" and
             today of all days, you lot have to be the ones to
             bloody get in my –

36

THOMAS slips – RICHARD and MATTHEW catch him.

RICHARD: Are you okay?

MATTHEW: All right?

THOMAS: I'm fine! I'm fine!

THOMAS catches sight of something.

THOMAS: I knew it. I knew it.

MATTHEW: *(To THOMAS.)* Look if…

RICHARD sees it.

RICHARD: Is that a person?

MATTHEW: Where?

MATTHEW sees it.

RICHARD: What is she doing?

THOMAS: You can see her too?

AYEESHA is stood is a strange position on a raised rock in the middle of field. The three men are stopped in their tracks.

MATTHEW: Hello!

RICHARD: Hey! You alright! *(She ignores them.)* You alright love!?!

MATTHEW: Hello!

RICHARD: Can she hear us?

MATTHEW: We almost didn't see you in the fog!

RICHARD: She can't hear us.

MATTHEW: It's likely to get a lot worse out here!

THOMAS: I don't understand.

MATTHEW: Can we help?

RICHARD: You need to come down!

MATTHEW: Do you know where you're going? …
                Thomas? She needs to come down doesn't
                she?

AYEESHA turns away.

THOMAS: Oh…

Beat.

RICHARD: Miss, why are you up there?

MATTHEW: Where do you want to get to?

RICHARD: We're walking! Are you walking?

THOMAS: You're here.

RICHARD: You've not even got the right attire!

MATTHEW: Perhaps you're parked nearby?

AYEESHA stands to her feet.

THOMAS: Oh! I'm sorry. I've worked as hard as I can…

Beat.

MATTHEW: I'm sorry but there's a serious weather
                warning!

RICHARD: A policeman warned us!

AYEESHA turns.

THOMAS: Please.

RICHARD: Please Madam…

MATTHEW: *(Indicating to weather and fog.)* It's dangerous.
                Look!

AYEESHA looks around. Pause. She points off down the hill. AYEESHA
goes back into her pose

RICHARD: She's crazy.

MATTHEW: Hm…But we can't leave her. Not like this.

THOMAS: Look lads, you go.

RICHARD: What?

THOMAS: Go. I'll take care of this

MATTHEW: I suppose you are the most experienced
                here. But you'll both need to get a move on.

THOMAS: Don't worry. *(THOMAS stares up at AYEESHA.)*

MATTHEW: Hey Thomas…Just make sure you come
                back, alright Tom?… Tom?

THOMAS: You take the path down. I'll catch you up.

MATTHEW: Right – agreed.

RICHARD: Okay. Good luck.

RICHARD and THOMAS leave.

THOMAS waits.

THOMAS: I know why you're here.

Pause. AYEESHA comes out of the pose.

THOMAS: I know why you're here.

AYEESHA: Really?

THOMAS: Yes.

Beat.

AYEESHA: Do you know me?

THOMAS:	Well, no… but… Ha! I was right!
AYEESHA:	Good for you.
THOMAS:	You're the reason I'm out here.
AYEESHA:	What?
THOMAS:	You're here for peace aren't you?
AYEESHA:	Hm.
THOMAS:	Sometimes you can't fight anymore.
AYEESHA:	… It was all too much. *(Beat.)* So now…
THOMAS:	So now?…
AYEESHA:	I'm being present.
THOMAS:	Of course! …Well, I'm here now.

Beat.

AYEESHA:	Will you stop staring!
THOMAS:	I didn't expect a girl but I'm here…for you. You brought me here.
AYEESHA:	Nah, thanks very much and everything, but didn't you hear your friends? …Go home…
THOMAS:	Oh. *(Beat.)* But if I could just connect with you, with all of you. I've ignored it for so long! Kept my head down and did the right thing y'know? But I always knew I'd be destined for great great things… Obviously, Administration and Resource Manager wasn't my plan A… But – then before, I was in the hallway and I had… What were we talking about?
AYEESHA:	I dunno. …Just go please.
THOMAS:	You're the key!

AYEESHA:	I don't know you!
THOMAS:	What do you want me to do?
AYEESHA:	Go away! I want to be ON. MY. OWN.
THOMAS:	Yes! That's it! So I'm HERE!
AYEESHA:	Erm, I don't think you get how it works... Just leave.
THOMAS:	Not after coming this far. It's time isn't it?
AYEESHA:	Yep. Time's up. Off you go random old guy, bye.

She returns to her meditative pose. Beat.

THOMAS:	I've been pushing my, my burdensome circle and retracing my steps. But today, I'm more present, more alive today than I've been in years!
AYEESHA:	Flippin' heck... Come on then. Are you alright mate? Seriously eh?
	We need to get you back. *(She starts to get down.)* Now where are your mates?
THOMAS:	Let me help you down.
AYEESHA:	Okay!
THOMAS:	*(Goes to help.)* Here.
AYEESHA:	I can do it.
THOMAS:	Careful. It's slippery.
AYEESHA:	I know what it is! *(She climbs down.)* Which way down? Let's get you back to your friends.
THOMAS:	This way down.
AYEESHA:	You just stay where I can see you okay?

41

ACT TWO

SCENE ONE

All four characters are now walking together, weaving between stones on the way downhill.

AYEESHA: So it's not just you on your jones then?

MATTHEW: Normally there's more us.

RICHARD: Sometimes up to thirty of us.

AYEESHA: And you're all black?

MATTHEW: Yes.

AYEESHA: Men?

MATTHEW: It's exhilarating.

AYEESHA: And you do this every month?

RICHARD: Well, I actually missed last month because I was away.

MATTHEW: Star Trek convention.

AYEESHA: Obviously.

RICHARD: Be careful Ayeesha, the stones are wet here. *(Beat.)* You were lucky we came across you!

AYEESHA: Yeah, glory be.

MATTHEW: What brought you out here?

AYEESHA: It just got a little hectic.

RICHARD: Exactly! That's why we come out here. A bit of greenery –

MATTHEW:	Yes, it can get a bit much.
AYEESHA:	But it's kinda odd in't it? You being out here.
MATTHEW:	*(To AYEESHA.)* Well, you're here…
RICHARD:	Why do you think that it's odd?
AYEESHA:	Apart from the weather?
RICHARD:	Apart from the weather.
AYEESHA:	Um… Black people really live in the cities, innit though? Countryside's not for us. I don't get it. …
MATTHEW:	It's a safe space you see?
AYEESHA:	Safe space! I wouldn't like to go in a pub round here.
MATTHEW:	Oh, I think you'll find it's not like that anymore. Not round here anyway. We're just black men… Walking in the countryside –
AYEESHA:	Walk into one those pubs and you'd be black men running.
MATTHEW:	No, it's quite pleasant now.
RICHARD:	We can go where we like now.
AYEESHA:	Can you really?
RICHARD:	What you need to understand, is some people think we're the group who are most likely to be involved with crime and drugs. Think we're thugs on the street, gangsters, always hustling and killing ourselves –
AYEESHA:	I don't think anyone is thinking THAT about YOU guys.

RICHARD:	– when in actual fact, we're out here on a walk bettering ourselves!
AYEESHA:	Black on black walking? …Genius. Sounds… like you're achieving a lot! You get badges yeah?
RICHARD:	No, no. We walk out our identity.
MATTHEW:	Y-Yes. Exactly!
AYEESHA:	Walk out your what? What's that meant to mean?
RICHARD:	Our identity! The only way to be who you truly are, is to be true to yourself, yes?
AYEESHA:	Okay.
RICHARD:	So, how can you can be true to yourself, if you don't know who you are?
AYEESHA:	*(To RICHARD.)* And who are you? Countryfile? …I'm freezing.
THOMAS:	I've got an extra fleece it you'd like –
AYEESHA:	Nah, you're alright. Are you sure this isn't just a fancy way to mess up your trainers?
RICHARD:	No no. You see, Malcolm X said: "There's a new type of black man who wants to speak for himself, stand on his own feet, and WALK for himself." It means WE define who we are. We walk.
MATTHEW:	Right!
AYEESHA:	Really? Brilliant. And what yeah? Did Martin Luther King have a dream too? Amazing.

RICHARD:	No, actually what I'm trying to say is that it's not other people that define you. You decide who you are!
AYEESHA:	And you think that works?
RICHARD:	Aha... W.E.B Dubois writes about a double consciousness? You know YOU are yourself. But they... don't see you as you. You see? They just see their prejudices. They place another identity on you. They look at you differently because you're African-Caribbean right?
AYEESHA:	Maybe.
RICHARD:	So you are consciously looking at yourself through your own eyes, AND through the eyes of society. So we are in our own culture, and the British culture at the same time. Walking between two selves! And between these two, we as black people have to walk this path where we have the opportunities to see many things that others may not! Have you thought about THAT?
AYEESHA:	What do you mean our "own" culture?
RICHARD:	Who we are.
AYEESHA:	But haven't they pushed us all into the same culture anyway? All like, these different people, are just lumped in as 'black'. They won. We lost.
RICHARD:	...Maybe. But that is the double consciousness. Walking two identities. Being black AND being British. A double consciousness.
MATTHEW:	Yes! Double consciousness.
AYEESHA:	Yeah, well I'm a woman – so that's triple consciousness.

MATTHEW:	Oh, right.
RICHARD:	But we can choose to create our identity. Actually we are empowered! You are empowered!
MATTHEW:	We walk.
RICHARD:	We walk.
THOMAS:	So we walk.
AYEESHA:	Whatever. Totally normal. A bunch of black guys walking around trying to find yourselves in your Berghaus and your North Face. ...Did you lot really have to run into me while you were having your black life crisis?

Beat.

	...I knew I should've stayed by myself.
MATTHEW:	And what do you do?
AYEESHA:	I'm an MC.
THOMAS:	An MC!
RICHARD:	You're a rapper?
AYEESHA:	Yeah.
MATTHEW:	Oh. Have you released anything?
AYEESHA:	Not yet. Just working with some producers –
MATTHEW:	Right.
RICHARD:	What's your 'professional' name?
MATTHEW:	Your stage name? No, I mean your rap name? Your... Hip-Hop moniker?
AYEESHA:	Ayeesha.

Beat.

MATTHEW: Oh...

THOMAS: Right.

AYEESHA: It's me, int' it? Keep it real.

(Beat. MATTHEW's phone goes off.)

MATTHEW: Sorry. *(Checks text.)*

THOMAS: *(To AYEESHA.)* A rapper?... Well, I didn't expect
                  that. *(Beat.)* Out here.

RICHARD: I remember when I first came here there was
                  that big hit with Ja Rule featuring that singer
                  Ashanti. Have you heard of her?

AYEESHA: Yeah, 'course.

RICHARD: You know she's not even Ashanti! No
                  connection to Ghana whatsover! ...Just some
                  puffed up rappers telling us about how much
                  "dough" they have, dressed up like clowns!

AYEESHA: I don't listen to much of that old skool stuff
                  anyway.

MATTHEW: Old school? Ja Rule!?!

RICHARD: What I want to know is where's that political
                  message nowadays?

MATTHEW: Ah yes... KRS-One. Gangstarr. Ice Cube.
                  NWA, brilliant...

AYEESHA: You liked them??? Hold up. YOU were into
                  Hip-Hop?

MATTHEW: Yes.

AYEESHA: You used to listen to NWA?

MATTHEW:	And obviously Chuck D. Public Enemy.
RICHARD:	Ah, yes The Public Enemy… But you know, I always liked soul music – "What's Going On?" Marvin Gaye. Ayeesha, you won't know that one will you? It's a very good one, it goes *(Sings.)* 'Motha, motha, there's far too may of you –'
AYEESHA:	I know it. Look –
RICHARD:	But what message are you… *(MATTHEW's phone goes.)*
MATTHEW:	Sorry. I've got to –
AYEESHA:	Who keeps texting you?
MATTHEW:	Just home.
RICHARD:	I thought it was work?
MATTHEW:	I'd better… *(Composes text.)*
RICHARD:	*(To AYEESHA.)* Consider this, what are you putting out there into the world, for the next generation, y'know?
AYEESHA:	I am the next generation! What have you done? Have you thought about THAT?
RICHARD:	Ah, you see we are actively asserting our right to be here. Isn't that right Thomas? We walk our history. Woodlands. The earth. We walk. We connect to the environment. Nature.
MATTHEW:	*(Texting.)* Yes, so many of us seem so disconnected from it.
RICHARD:	But we ARE nature. We walk from nature to nature.
AYEESHA:	No mate. You lot are men. *I'M* nature.

RICHARD:	We're claiming this land as ours aren't we Thomas?
AYEESHA:	What does that even mean?
MATTHEW:	It's a political act!
AYEESHA:	Really now? I'd LOVE to know how.
RICHARD:	This is our home!
AYEESHA:	Where you from again?
RICHARD:	Actually I have a right to be here. I heard to be a Yorkshireman, you have to live here at least fifteen years. And I've been here since 1997!

AYEESHA stops.

AYEESHA:	No disrespect yeah? But you lot are stupid...
MATTHEW:	Well –
AYEESHA:	Is that all you do then... walk?
RICHARD:	Is that all you do then... rap?
AYEESHA:	Wow, thanks for sorting everything in the world guys. By starting a walking group. ...Perfect. You don't know anything about my world or what I been through.
MATTHEW:	Well, we're getting you back to your car aren't we?
AYEESHA:	Are you? You know what? I know who I am at least!
RICHARD:	Then why were you lost in a place you don't even know, standing on a rock in the freezing cold wearing clothes that are not even water-resistant!

AYEESHA: Cos I'm made of stronger stuff than all of you
                put together. That's why! Simple. Posh boy,
                trekkie and old man weirdo? You're the ones
                who seem a bit lost to me!

                I can't be bothered with this! I'll see you later.
                (AYEESHA storms off on ahead.) And make sure
                HE *(Indicating THOMAS.)* doesn't come after me!

MATTHEW: Hold on! Don't go! You don't know the way.

RICHARD: Outrageous! What's got her knickers in a twist?

Beat.

THOMAS: She's right.

MATTHEW: Come back! We'd better go after her.

RICHARD: Really?

MATTHEW: Come on guys. Before we lose her.

                (MATTHEW leaves first, followed by RICHARD.)

THOMAS: She's right. *(Beat. He laughs.)*

SCENE TWO.

*AYEESHA stands in a queue in an inner-city chicken shop 9:30 p.m. the
night before.*

AYEESHA: *(Rap.)*
                I'm not sure really, what am I gonna eat?
                …look up at the menu in front of me
                Some popcorn chicken, zinger box, deluxe
                feast?
                …Or fries and two piece?

                A few of my mates, we was out on a rave
                But now it's just me…

50

I can't decide what I'm havin'
Zinger Tower Fillet with cheese just nyam it

Normally I'm not a girl who's out on my own
'specially on Friday night on City Road
But I got the car and on my way home
Thought I'd get Hotwings …wait …oh?

(Spoken.)
Can I have the Boxmeal with the hotwings
please?

(Rap.)
Take my food and sit down in the restaurant
Take a quick pic and Instagram it
After the food is devoured …
Spot my old friend Cazza working behind the
counter

She's a sweet girl, thought that I'd shout her
There's still a queue, so I walk around but
I'm waiting to say 'Hi'… just as I was I about ta
Something happens to mash up the encounter.

Some nugget in the queue starts running his
mouth off
Getting louder… y'know, just like a lout does
A bit drunk, thinks I'm cutting in front – mista
big stuff
Turns and he says "Get to the back of the queue
nig nog..."
Get to the back of the queue nig nog?
Get to the back of the queue nig nog?

And all of the place – silent, as if things about to
kick off
…And you know what?
(Not bars.)

51

I just laughed at him. For real. I just laughed at him.

(Rap.)
Is that the best you can do? ...Somebody tell him please
Those your best words? Your words ain't threatening
'Nig Nog?' ...What's this the Seventies???
'Nig Nog' sounds stupid. It doesn't sound menacing

Of all the racist insults you could've involved
... "Nig nog?" You chose THAT one?... Oh...
That's interesting. I'm not sure it really works?
You're such a simpleton: you slur your slurs

(Spoken.)
He's looking a bit shook now.

(Rap.)
Did you think you were gonna scare me – I'd tremble and leg it?
Even your ignorance is ignorant
Even your terrible ATTEMPT at offensive
Is offensive... Even your dis is dis-credited

(Not bars.)
He mumbles something about there's too many of me now? Like blah, blah, blah...

(Rap.)
Nah, Then listen
Yes, I'm dark and Yorkshire! – Hendersons' relish
Don't you ever forget it,
I'm Beyonce with lemonade – that makes you a lemon

52

So dead it. You talk bish – you should be buried
Thinking you're rebellious being racist? – cos
John Terry said it?
Nah then – hell of a thing
You just got burnt. Is that cos you got no
melanin?
…Maaaate.

(Rap.)
Behind the counter my mate Cazza… just has ta
Laugh and react ta the whole incident as it
happens
The drunk idiot, inches toward where I'm
standing
I think if he swings… I'll just lamp him

And the manager's laughing too
The idiot is still radged, but the lad's on mute
Thinking I'd better move, let the guy grab his
food
And I'll head back to Sharla's for a brew

I turn away… He steps out my face
Take a deep breath, the adrenalin fades
Sit down and have the realization
That really, I coulda got seriously brayed
What a night!… weird
Then this guy's mate turns round and sneers
He says: "Why don't you go back to your own
country
You're not welcome here.

This is a white country, it's my country
We don't want no immigrants in
So get out of the shop with your chicken and
chips
We only speak English here."

(Not bars.)
And for some reason it all hits me when I leave the shop. Get into my car and start to drive. Turn on the radio. It's Toddla T. "Fiya!" And I'm crying.

SCENE THREE

MATTHEW is alone in the fog looking for AYEESHA.

MATTHEW: Hello! Hello! We're over here! *(Beat.)* Ayeesha!

(Phone bleeps with text message. He reads it.)

Oh, come on. *(Typing response.)* "I – am – not – arguing – over – text." Send.

(He sends message.)

(Beat.)

(He gets a new message and reads it. AYEESHA begins to arrive.)

Because Vicky! I can't fit what I want to say into a bloody text message!... Oh... "Please darling – smiley face – I am..."

AYEESHA: Hey, I'm here...

MATTHEW: There you are! Great.

AYEESHA: Sorry, looked like you were in a private moment.

MATTHEW: Ah, it just my wife. Just... um... Just hang on.

　　(MATTHEW keeps texting.)

AYEESHA: Where's the other two? Can't see anything in this.

It's as if the clouds have come down over us.
Like we're walking in a cloud.
You texting for help or somemut?

MATTHEW: Sorry... Oh no. She's just away with the kids at the moment.

AYEESHA: Not walking then?

MATTHEW: Er... We'd be better get back.

AYEESHA: Right.

MATTHEW: The guys should just be over there.

MATTHEW and AYEESHA walk on.

AYEESHA: So does your wife ever come on these "Claiming your land" walks or is it just for men?

MATTHEW: Just for men.

AYEESHA: Really? Just for men? That's really forward thinking of you.

MATTHEW: No, it's not like that – it's a break from home, you know...

AYEESHA: So you can moan about your wife? As if black women haven't got enough –

MATTHEW: She's white...

AYEESHA: Ah.

MATTHEW: This is for us... To – to explore our roots.

AYEESHA: In the Peak District? Are you from here?

MATTHEW: Uh, no...

AYEESHA: Well, I guess you married a white woman and you're still together. That's impressive.

MATTHEW:	Do you have family?
AYEESHA:	"Do you have family!" What kind of question is that? No, I just dropped out of the sky and formed out of your primeval rib!
MATTHEW:	Er... sorry.

Beat.

AYEESHA:	...I live with my mum and my little brother. *(Beat.)* ...Manor Top.
MATTHEW:	Right.
AYEESHA:	Fit in with your cliché stereotype? Running off in the middle of an argument, yeah?
MATTHEW:	Oh no, oh no...
AYEESHA:	What do you do? Job, I mean.
MATTHEW:	I'm a doctor.
AYEESHA:	Okay... Right then, so how did you get into Hip-Hop?
MATTHEW:	Oh well... I think it was Vicky actually.
AYEESHA:	Your wife?
MATTHEW:	Yes, I was at university and she took me to my first Public Enemy concert. Powerful stuff. The message. The image. The sheer sound of it. I was into it from then really.
AYEESHA:	Yeah, they're hard still.
MATTHEW:	You listen to Public Enemy?
AYEESHA:	'Course. – "Elvis was a hero to most ...

MATTHEW & AYEESHA:	*(Start to rap in style of Chuck D.)* "but he never mean shhh to me, straight up racist that sucker was simple and plain –
MATTHEW:	*(In style of Flava Fav.)* "Mother *'Bleep'* him and John Wayne!"

They laugh.

MATTHEW:	I quite like Elvis actually.
AYEESHA:	Me too.
MATTHEW:	When get home, I'll have to dig it out that track and play it to my lads.
AYEESHA:	What are your kids called, sorry – "Do you have family?"
MATTHEW:	Ha… Kieran and Jack.
AYEESHA:	Bet your rayt glad they're not out today.
MATTHEW:	Yes… I'm hopeful that, perhaps when they're older… You want them to grow up with a strong sense of self, their heritage and so on. So they're prepared for the… That's one of the reason we come on these walks.
AYEESHA:	How old are they?
MATTHEW:	Both secondary now… How old's your little brother?
AYEESHA:	Benji's ten. Right little scamp he is.
MATTHEW:	Right.
AYEESHA:	Nah, he's cool actually. It's just getting him ready for school in the mornings.
MATTHEW:	Oh yes. I'm familiar with that one.

AYEESHA:	God knows what sense of identity or whatever he'll have though... There are a lot of idiots out there. ...Where do you live?
MATTHEW:	Fullwood... Near Stumperlowe House?
AYEESHA:	I think your lads'll be fine mate.

Beat.

MATTHEW:	Well, I'm sure his big sister will be a good influence... With your creative talents.
AYEESHA:	Yeah, it's either that or Jewellery.
MATTHEW:	Sorry?
AYEESHA:	I'm in my second year doing Jewellery and Metalwork design. It's alright actually. Just want to show Benji you can achieve innit? I don't want him to be afraid to be someone. People still put us in a box.
MATTHEW:	Not everyone though. It is the 21st century after all. Perhaps we make it too complicated. I mean black people are really assimilated into culture now. A lot of progress has been made –
AYEESHA:	Really. Wake up.
MATTHEW:	Well I think I'm awake, but if we bring up race all the time –
AYEESHA:	All the time?
MATTHEW:	Look, some would say by holding onto past hostilities we're actually creating more barriers which will only have negative consequences for the future.
AYEESHA:	Right, it's my own fault?
MATTHEW:	Well, no – that's not what they're saying.

AYEESHA:	Like there's not racism anymore? Are you dizzy?
MATTHEW:	I'm just presenting a point of view.
AYEESHA:	And if someone racially abuses me, I should just suck it up?
MATTHEW:	No. But she says – I mean, the point is if we focus on what separates us –
AYEESHA:	Ah, there's only one race isn't there?
MATTHEW:	In a way –
AYEESHA:	So I can't be proud of who I am? And the fact I'm British?
MATTHEW:	I – I think what she's saying is –
AYEESHA:	Oh right.
MATTHEW:	I –
AYEESHA:	You know what Matthew? I think I know your wife.
MATTHEW:	Really? I don't think so…
AYEESHA:	Pretty sure I do. She liked black guys right? *(Beat.)* Just not TOO black.
MATTHEW:	You don't know the first thing about –
AYEESHA:	*(Kisses teeth.)* …You'd better text her back, Tupac.
MATTHEW:	I'm not talking to you about this. Now where are Thomas and Richard?
AYEESHA:	Yeah, yeah. She's away with the kids. Right. *(Beat.)* You know what Matthew, for a doctor and all that, you're pretty dumb. Call her and

talk to her properly. Let her know how you're
feeling, y'know?

MATTHEW: I'm not talking to you about this... You're
young, you don't understand... *(Shouts.)*
Thomas! ...She just needs some space.

AYEESHA: Her mum's?

MATTHEW: Her sister's... *(Shouts.)* Richard!

AYEESHA: ...And you went on a walk.

Beat.

MATTHEW: Come on.

They walk toward the sound.

AYEESHA: So when you've been out here thinking about
your roots and that. Proper going in –

MATTHEW: I think I can hear them over there.

AYEESHA: Where's she in all this eh? Bet she's the one
who thinks she's in the middle of a wilderness.

MATTHEW: Come on. I'm still not talking about this. Here
they are...

(THOMAS and RICHARD arrive.)

AYEESHA: Great. Black Last of the Summer Wine.

THOMAS: You're here! Sorry lass, but we better get
moving, otherwise we'll be jiggered. Put this on
(Getting AYEESHA a spare fleece from his bag.)

MATTHEW: Which way from here Thomas?

They stop.

THOMAS: Right. Well...

AYEESHA:	You don't know do ya?
THOMAS:	I'm sure we'll all be back in the caff in no time. I'll buy you a cuppa, eh lass?
AYEESHA:	Just get me to my car thanks.
MATTHEW:	This doesn't look that familiar Thomas.
THOMAS:	Look, there's that style. This is where we met the policeman.
RICHARD:	No it isn't.

Beat.

AYEESHA:	Oh God.
MATTHEW:	It's just the fog. I think if we retrace our steps.
THOMAS:	No, I know the way. We've got to push through. Get to the woods.
RICHARD:	We're alright Thomas, yes?
THOMAS:	Oh God. *(He looks up at the atmosphere.)* They're doing it again. Bet the forecast didn't say owt about this!
MATTHEW:	About what? What's wrong?
THOMAS:	Feel that?
RICHARD:	Eh?
AYEESHA:	What?
THOMAS:	Snow.

ACT THREE

SCENE ONE

All of a sudden a snowsquall has descended. The characters march through blizzard conditions. THOMAS followed by AYEESHA, RICHARD and MATTHEW lagging behind.

MATTHEW: Thomas!

THOMAS: Come on lass.

MATTHEW: Hold on, it's slippery.

RICHARD: Okay!

MATTHEW: Thomas! Where are you?

THOMAS: This way! ...Not much further! Stay close!

AYEESHA: Okay.

MATTHEW: I can't see the tree line!

RICHARD: What?

MATTHEW: I can't see the tree line! No sign of the woods!

THOMAS: *(To the ANCESTORS.)* Show us the way! I can't go yet! At least let me lead them out of here before I go!

AYEESHA: What?

THOMAS: *(To the ANCESTORS.)* Show me!

RICHARD: Across here!

MATTHEW: Hold on!

THOMAS:	Watch out on the way down here. These rocks aren't steady.

They all stop at a river crossing that has been completely flooded. THOMAS gazes across the waters.

RICHARD:	Where are we?
THOMAS:	There's no way through! Bridge has gone.
RICHARD:	Are we heading the right way Thomas?
MATTHEW:	Gone? We should be at the woods by now… Even if we had taken the wrong trail. We'd have hit a road by now at least –
AYEESHA:	This is a great walking group innit? Have you not even got maps or a compass or something?
MATTHEW:	We have Thomas, he will know the way.
AYEESHA:	He dun't know what day it is if you ask me.
MATTHEW:	Thomas? *(Silence.)* Thomas? How far to Padley Gorge now? We can't see anything. You okay Tom? Perhaps, you should have some water?
RICHARD:	Yes. Keep hydrated.

(MATTHEW gives THOMAS some water.)

AYEESHA:	Who were you talking to back there Thomas?
RICHARD:	*(To MATTHEW.)* Do you know the way?
MATTHEW:	*(To RICHARD.)* No. And Thomas isn't well.
RICHARD:	Matthew, where's your phone?
MATTHEW:	Here. *(Looking at phone.)* There's not enough signal for maps.
RICHARD:	Lets call 999. Right?

MATTHEW: Well…

AYEESHA: You guys calling for help?

RICHARD: Yes.

MATTHEW: Yes. *(MATTHEW dials.)*

AYEESHA: I can't believe this.

(They wait. The phonecall is cut off.)

RICHARD: Reception?

MATTHEW: It's dead.

RICHARD: No.

AYEESHA: You lot are a joke. Yeah, you've walked your
              identity out. Out into the middle of a flipping
              snowstorm! *(THOMAS hasn't moved.)* Thomas.

(Beat.)

MATTHEW: Tom?

RICHARD: Oh no.

Silence.

THOMAS: They're everywhere.

Beat.

AYEESHA: Who's he keep talking to? Have you heard
              him?

RICHARD: *(To MATTHEW.)* How long have you known this?
              And you still went on this walk?

MATTHEW: How was I supposed to know? He seemed
              alright.

RICHARD: We shouldn't have come out. Matthew, we should've gone straight back...

MATTHEW: Who are you talking to, Tom?

THOMAS: *(To group pointing off into the fog.)* You don't see them?

MATTHEW: Who?

THOMAS: It's this way... Follow me. You've gotta follow me... Let's go.

THOMAS gets up to leave.

MATTHEW: Thomas...

THOMAS: I can see it. Come on.

RICHARD: What? We can't go up there!

AYEESHA: Does he always do this?

MATTHEW: No. Hey Thomas! If you go that way I won't follow you.

THOMAS: *(To ANCESTORS far off.)* Wait! *(To group.)* C'mon!

THOMAS leaves.

RICHARD: We've got no idea what's up there. He'll get us killed!

AYEESHA: Well come on, we can't just leave him to it and let him go.

MATTHEW: No don't. It's insanity!

AYEESHA: Hold up, Thomas!

MATTHEW: Don't – *(He grabs her arm.)*

AYEESHA: Seriously? Get off me.

MATTHEW lets go. AYEESHA follows after THOMAS. MATTHEW and RICHARD don't move.

RICHARD: I'm not going up there. …You should've done something earlier – We should be going THAT way. *(Indicating another direction.)*

MATTHEW: Look, it's not my fault. If they're going off on their own, it's best you and I stay together. Okay Richard? Look I'm not going up there, I've got a family to get back to.

RICHARD: What about the brotherhood?

MATTHEW: I'm also a father alright? You won't underst… Look, we'll try and get help. If we keep heading down way, this I sure it'll will take us toward civilisation.

RICHARD: You're sure this is the right thing to do?

(Beat.)

MATTHEW: I think so. *(MATTHEW makes to leave.)*

RICHARD: Even when he's gone. *(Into the ether.)* Bastard!

(RICHARD follows.)

WE WALK PART 5

ANCESTORS: We walk
We walk
We walk
And SHE walks
The young girl
Caught before her time
Trapped in time

Before the circus owner

66

Before the miller
Before...
SHE walks
4th century
The African princess

The Bangled lady
A woman in but still in her youth
Here in God's country
The cosmopolitan hub of the northern
territories
She lies adorned

Arms interlaced with bracelets of two materials
Of Ivory from the African elephant
And the Jet gemstone from Whitby on the
Yorkshire coast
To the heart of Yorkshire
Here in a bitter white winter
Like a forgotten folk story
She can walk no longer.
Near the sycamore trees
Jet and ivory
Death
Lying with sisters from every age
The burial casket reading
Soror ave vivas in deo' –
'Sister, farewell, may you live in God.'
Return to us.

SCENE TWO

AYEESHA catches up with THOMAS.

AYEESHA: Hiya, bit nippy out in't it?

THOMAS:	*(Laughing.)*... I like you. Not to worry, I'll get you out of this.
AYEESHA:	Don't know where the others are. Head back yeh?
THOMAS:	You've just got to trust me now. We haven't got long.
AYEESHA:	Where are you taking us?
THOMAS:	I'm not taking you anywhere – it's them. I'm just following.
AYEESHA:	Who? There's no one there.
THOMAS:	*(Laughing.)* I know you can see them! I knew you'd come. You can see can't ya!
AYEESHA:	What are you on about? I can hardly see owt!
THOMAS:	Stick close. We follow them.
AYEESHA:	No. Enough, right? Listen we need to get back. Stop!

THOMAS stops.

	Let's just go home. yeah?
THOMAS:	We are home. This is our home, don't you see? Our ancestors. It's taken me that long to accept it. I know I'm living in shadows now. We're all living in shadows. I'm halfway to being a shadow myself. I knew there was just one last thing I had to do... They're calling us. Come on.

They walk on.

AYEESHA:	What are you on about?
THOMAS:	Our ancestors! Our forbears they're here!

68

AYEESHA: Not mine. Where are you going?

THOMAS: Yes. All of our forebears. It's why we're here. …
             Let me just say something… Is that okay?

AYEESHA: Alright.

THOMAS: Not far from where we are, is the Roman Road.
             And further along over there is Fenny Lane.
             These are ancient trackways, you see? Once
             these roads were established all sorts would've
             used them. And these figures from history
             would've have walked where we walk. We'd be
             passers-by! On the exact same path we're on
             now. Think of it. Black Yorkshire! We've had
             black people here for centuries.

AYEESHA: Black Yorkshire?

*They have entered the woods. The wind has died down. The mist thins
a little. Snowflakes flutter from the branches above.*

THOMAS: Look.

AYEESHA: Trees.

THOMAS: Padley Gorge.

AYEESHA: It's beautiful.

THOMAS: It's alright love… Careful. Mind your feet, it's
             icy… We should be alright now. Not far.

They walk.

AYEESHA: Thomas?

THOMAS: Yes.

AYEESHA: So Moors… they're black people right? Is that
             why it's called a moor?

THOMAS: No.

AYEESHA: Oh.

Beat.

THOMAS: But you see don't you? We're still here. Even
                when we're gone. We're still here. Ayeesha
                listen.

AYEESHA: Yeah.

THOMAS: You are MEANT to be here. Look...

THOMAS sits under a tree with large roots, AYEESHA joins him sitting.

                Let's get this snow off.

*THOMAS brushes snow off base of tree, AYEESHA helps, a tree revealing
a huge millstone.*

AYEESHA: A millstone.

THOMAS: See, it's become part of that tree...

AYEESHA: The roots have grown all over –

Beat.

THOMAS: Yes... Centuries! They've been here since the
                1700s at least! Like our history. Worked into the
                earth. These stones...

AYEESHA: Yeah, we were slaves right?...

THOMAS: Oh no! That's what they tell you, there's so
                much more! We can go before that! We were
                HERE before that! We can go back to I dunno,
                1600s – John Moore, the black businessman in
                York. He may even have paid for some of those
                millstones to be quarried, y'know?

AYEESHA: Great, so there was one black British guy. Great.

THOMAS: Noooo! Henry the Eighth! –

AYEESHA:	He was white. Fact. And he was a ginger. Everyone knows th –
THOMAS:	Ah, but Henry's first wife. Catherine of Aragon –
AYEESHA:	– that ended well.
THOMAS:	Yeah. Well, Catherine had a trumpet playing royal attendant – "John Blanke" an African man. He'd have mostly likely been on their royal progresses up to Pontefract Castle – Yorkshire!

ANCESTORS slowly appear and dissolve and appear as THOMAS and AYEESHA speak.

ANCESTORS & THOMAS:	– We Walk…
THOMAS:	– and he could've passed through here. A musician – like you eh? Think of it!
ANCESTORS:	The trumpet herald. His figure is inscribed upon time-worn membranes Woven together. Beneath royal banners – Breath enters *(They blow.)* And…
AYEESHA:	But we're not exactly FROM here are we?
ANCESTORS:	Noise is heard.
AYEESHA:	We're not really English are we?
THOMAS:	Are we not? How long do we have to be here to be English?
ANCESTORS:	We speak.

THE ANCESTORS move with THOMAS.

THOMAS:	Look, I told you about the Roman Road didn't I? There was a Roman outpost just near here. Imagine Roman Emperor Septimus Severus passing through here? An African. 200 AD.
AYEESHA:	Crazy.
THOMAS:	And after Septimus' death, his son made Ebocoram – York, capital of the North of England. So really, if you think about it, it was an African that put the York in Yorkshire! And I'm not even counting the countless others after – all sorts of Africans – Black people in England. The Georgians, the Tudors... We were here before the Anglo-Saxons! You see? Generations upon generations. Right down to my Dad who worked in the Sheffield Steelworks! You see? We've left our imprint on the earth here, in nature. We are here!
	This is why you've been sent to me now. Sitting here listening to me! This land is ours too. We are Yorkshire. We are Britain.
ANCESTORS:	Some of us thought that we would die here Others rejoiced that we –

ANCESTORS dissolve as AYEESHA cuts them off.

AYEESHA:	The thing is, you're putting your own meaning on it aren't ya? Your feelings on it. You might think it's important. But no one else does. Schools don't teach you that.
THOMAS:	Exactly. And why is that?
AYEESHA:	And if it's all true and everything, what's the point?
THOMAS:	But if you can see the past, you can –

AYEESHA: It doesn't stop my little brother finding racist
               stickers on our bus stop last year. It doesn't stop
               my mate Sharla getting called 'Paki' in broad
               daylight on Division Street after college! Or last
               night, when two scumbags call me "nig nog"
               and get right in my face and tell me to leave the
               country while everyone around me does sod
               all!

THOMAS: That happened to you?

AYEESHA: Yes it did. Funnily enough, the idea of a Tudor
               flippin' trumpet attendant didn't seem quite so
               relevant! I just drove and drove until I got out
               here. And now you! You? You're talking to the
               'shadow spirits'!?!

THOMAS: So you do see them!

AYEESHA: No!

THOMAS: Those spirits are the reason we are here. That's
               why you've got to listen. A silent fanfare…

AYEESHA: And why would they talk to you Thomas?
               Seems to me the only thing those ancestors
               had going for them was that they actually
               DID something! Walking? What the heck
               is that? You got too scared and then totally
               accepted what society told you haven't you?
               Just kept your heads down didn't ya? Bought
               a nice house, got comfortable and told your
               kids to work twice as hard as everyone else.
               Then everything will be fine. History? That's
               not real! You know what's real? The fact that
               you should've dealt with all this crap back in
               the day, but you walked away didn't did you?
               Cowards!

AYEESHA hears something and looks around to see a figure off in the mist.

What's that? ...Who's there on the other bank?
Hello! Hello????...Oh no, no, no...

She turns back to THOMAS who has disappeared.

Thomas? ...Thomas! Thomas!

THOMAS groans. He has slipped from the path, down the side of the gorge, and is holding onto the side. Perilously close to falling. He's holding onto to the undergrowth but it's coming away.

AYEESHA: I'm climbing down. Give me your hand...

THOMAS: No don't... It's okay. Part of me knew... Thank
             you. I knew when I saw you that you'd lead me
             here. It's right... Leave me. It's okay. They're
             all with me here. Right now. ...You just go find
             the lads. You take them home.

AYEESHA: Don't you be stupid there Thomas!

THOMAS: I'm going!

AYEESHA: Hold on! Help! Help!

AYEESHA struggles to hold on, THOMAS is about to fall. Suddenly MATTHEW and RICHARD arrive.

MATTHEW: Tom!

MATTHEW and RICHARD climb down to try and rescue THOMAS.

             Hang on!

RICHARD: It's not secure!

MATTHEW: It's not working! It's coming away! I can't find
             any grip! *(Slowly sliding down.)* I'm slipping! I'm
             slipping!

The rescue attempt falters and it ends up with the three men are linked and are suspended below AYEESHA with THOMAS at the bottom. AYEESHA attempts to reach down.

MATTHEW:	We're too heavy.
RICHARD:	We're going to fall!
THOMAS:	They're calling. Let me go.
AYEESHA:	NO! I am MEANT to be here! *(To ANCESTORS.)* Come on then! WE WALK!

WE WALK PART 6

AYEESHA joins the WE WALK PART 6.

ANCESTORS: All of time is slipping.
Into the same land
The same rock
The same rivers
Under the same stars
Under the same disparate blackness

Woven through these Ridings

Some of us thought that we would die here

We cannot turn back
We do not walk alone
We have seen centuries

Now
We walk
In footsteps
The unremembered blood of elders gathered in
her veins
Summoning the war cry of a thousand heroes
and heroines all at once

The Spirits of the ANCESTORS fill AYEESHA and for a moment she possesses superhuman strength and as the poem continues she begins to pull.

We face our true selves
Each step we take toward unity
Each step toward liberty
Each step turns the ground into

AYEESHA: Home…

Silence.

You owe me a cup of tea Tom.

Beat.

RICHARD: Well you're in luck sis, as I happen to know
there's a particularly nice café at Grindleford.

Beat.

THOMAS: …They called you "nig nog"???

SCENE THREE

AYEESHA: *(Rap.)* It's two months on from that mad day in March
– no forgettin' it
When things got peak like district, lost in cold
temperatures
Spirits and visions, reaching over the precipice
And they walk with me right now…

Through the doors of the big department store
Round the escalator, stop and I pause
Perfume counters, on the ground floor
Sign says: "Jewellery & Watches"
Through the glass display case, looking at the
options
The lady behind the counter, on her phone
texting
I interrupt and she looks at me like, y'know
negative

(Spoken.)

Hiya, I'd like one of those necklaces.

"Are you sure? …Isn't a bit expensive?"

Yes, thanks. I'm sure.

(Rap.)

She looks me up and down

And says "No offence, but don't mess me around

Your lot tend to waste my time – your sort."

Your lot tend to waste my time – your sort?

YOUR SORT? …YOUR SORT?

Now the question is, how do I answer?

Do I ignore it, or challenge her with a bit a banter

Or get up in her face and demand to see the manager?

"Your sort?"… This latest casually racist statement

But this time I've got two thousand years of history bouncing 'round my brain yeah?

And lessons I've learnt from the journey I've taken.

I could slate her, take her down! or politely educate her?

Persuade her, work with her, wait with her

Give insight, and maybe one day campaign with her!

I think for a second… and then I turn around and say to her…

"Fuck off."

WE WALK PART 7

All actors bring back the "We Walk" choral chant with the female actor providing a new melody. The music swings low as the actors go into last poem.

THE ANCESTORS: Some of us thought that we would die here
Others rejoiced that we did.
When we realise we are not ALMOST home.
We are home.

We thought we would die
But you pushed me on, pulled me forth

There we are
Walking overgrown ancient trackways
The GP
With his wife now
Hands clasped
While two sons race ahead of them
Jumping millstones

The computer programmer
Newly returned from a house in Achimota,
Accra
Where in a bedroom
At the back of a drawer
He discovered
The postcard
A father had kept

And the former Senior Administration and
Resource Manager
Now founder of the Sankofa Saturday school
Near Pittsmoor
Where every weekend fifteen young minds
explode
As they learn of fanfares
Top hats

Keyholders
Bangled ladies
A great multitude
In God's country

And we walk
Walking
Walking in the footsteps of
The sales assistant
The carer
The student
The teachers
The person in the chicken shop
Everyone in the place tonight!
That person sat next to you!
Breathing in a thousand histories

Space has always been here
Time has always been here
We have always been here!
And we...

Music picks up again and soars to fade.

Printed in the USA
CPSIA information can be obtained
at www.ICGtesting.com
LVHW020900171024
794056LV00002B/632

9 781350 264663